YOUR DAUGHTER'S JOURNEY
(Inspirational & Motivational) Quotes

By: Shatora R. Gaskin

© 2019 by Shatora R. Gaskin. All rights reserved.
Words Matter Publishing
P.O. Box 531
Salem, Il 62881
www.wordsmatterpublishing.com

No part of this publication may be reproduced, stored in a retrieval system, or transmitted in any way by any means—electronic, mechanical, photocopy, recording, or otherwise—without the prior permission of the copyright holder, except as provided by USA copyright law.

ISBN 13: 978-1-949809-40-4
ISBN 10: 1-949809-40-4

Library of Congress Catalog Card Number: 2019950955

DEDICATION

To my Mama, who molded me into the woman I am today. I love you!

Acknowledgments:

First and foremost, I want to thank the creator for blessing me with this success and with the gift of writing. I would like to thank all the special women in my life who have had a positive influence on me and kept me motivated throughout this process. Mommy and Grandma, I love you. I also would like to give thanks to all of those who believed in me when I didn't. Thank you.

"Even the toughest people cry, even the brightest star gets dull."

Interpretation:
Nobody is perfect.

"Whoever said words don't hurt must have been deaf."

Interpretation:
Words do hurt and can really affect someone's feelings. Be considerate about what you say to others. Words hold weight. A person will always remember what you said to them, not only that but also how you made them feel.

"Life is like a vehicle, you're in control of the steering wheel. Along the ride you're going to come across some potholes, you're going to run over some boulders, but as long as you keep steering, you will see that the bumpy ride doesn't last long."

Interpretation:
You are in control of the path you choose to go down. You are in control of your life. Don't give up! Hang in there, and you will see there are better days ahead.

"After it rains, the sun always shines again,
and if it doesn't shine,
the sky still clears."

Interpretation:
Bad days won't last long..

"Never be afraid to go beyond your reach because you never know what you will grasp if you don't stretch your mind."

Interpretation:
Don't be afraid to go above and beyond to broaden your horizons because you never know what the outcome will be.

"People can take anything in the world from you. Except for your knowledge and wisdom, your awareness."

Interpretation:
Never let anyone change your way of thinking, your mind.

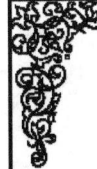

"Know what you want out of life and go get it, time waits for no one."

Interpretation:
Have a plan for yourself and work towards it. Don't wait!

"Only thing that can stop me is me, and I won't let myself down."

Interpretation:
Only you can hold yourself back from whatever it is you want to do in life.

"Nobody is going to hold you down the way yourself will."

Interpretation:
At the end of the day, you can only depend on yourself.

"There's a positive in every negative."

Interpretation:
In every bad situation there's a bright side.

"Everyone has a past, everyone has a story, and everyone has been through something. Nobody's life is perfect, it's all about moving forward. You can't dwell on what has already happened."

Interpretation:
Life happens for all of us, the only difference is how you react to it.

"Always stay true, you owe it to yourself."

Interpretation:
Be yourself and don't ever
change for anybody.

"Remain focused. Everything else will fall into place. Never force a thing. Whatever is meant to be will be."

Interpretation:
As long as you are giving your all and very best, things will start to fall into place as they should without you having to do anything.

"Only person I'm competing with is myself. I'm my worst enemy."

Interpretation:
Only person that can stop you is you. You always want to be better than you were the day before.

"If you woke up this morning, be thankful. Tomorrow isn't promised, you never know what can happen. Appreciate life. Some babies die the same day they're born. Be grateful."

Interpretation:
Cherish and be grateful for the little things. There's always someone in a worse situation than you, and somewhere in the world, there's someone that wishes they have what you have.

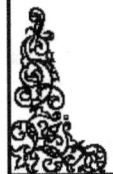 

"Never doubt yourself. You're more amazing than you know."

Interpretation:
Don't second guess yourself.
Take the risk, you'll be surprised what you can accomplish.

"Never let someone stop your hustle.
Your plan is your plan."

Interpretation:
Stick to your dream. Stick to your goals.
It's yours to manifest, no one else's.

"Life is serious, but not that serious."

Interpretation:
Don't be so hard on yourself. Laugh more!

"If you're not laughing, you're not living."
(Inspired by an old friend of mine).

Interpretation:
If there's no joy and humor in your life,
you are not living. Life's about happiness.

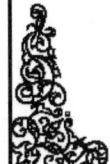

"You only live one time on Earth."

Interpretation:
Enjoy life while you have the chance.

"Smiles are contagious, remember that."

Interpretation:
By smiling, you can make someone else smile.

"Everything we are, everything we will be,
everything we want to be,
it all starts from inside."

Interpretation:
Our greatest creations and goal settings
start from within.

"Never be afraid to let your light shine."

Interpretation:
Be yourself with no hesitations.

"Life's a battlefield. You have to fight for what you deserve out of life and don't stop until you get it."

Interpretation:
Nothing in life comes easy. You have to fight for what you want and don't give up.

"If you don't understand life,
you'll be lost forever."

Interpretation:
If you don't know how life works, you
won't know how to live.

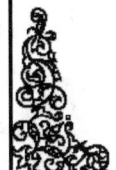 

"Never let your surroundings stop you from getting what you deserve out of life. The path is already paved for you, you're in control of the choices you make."

Interpretation:
It doesn't matter what neighborhood you live in or what town you grew up in, what matters is the choices you make from that point on to get to where you want to be in life.

"The grass is never greener on the other side. The glare from the sun just makes it look that way."

Interpretation:
Don't wish to be in someone else's shoes or situation because everything looks problem free. From the outside, you don't see the true color of things/people until you are deeply involved with them. Ironically you will discover that that situation is much worse than the one you're in. The grass is never greener on the other side.

"Life is what you make it."

Interpretation:
You are in control of the choices you make. You are responsible for the outcomes of your life.

"Don't be better, be different."

Interpretation:
Don't compete with others to be better.
Compete with yourself and be unique.
There's nothing better than being you.

"In every fine linen,
there's a crooked stitch."

Interpretation:
Nobody/nothing is perfect.

"Uncommon is always the most interesting."

Interpretation:
Anyone or anything that stands out that is different, that is unique draws more attention because it's not something you see every day.

"Love only not with your heart, but with your mind and soul."

Interpretation:
Don't just love. Love genuinely.

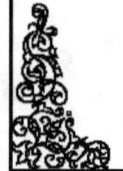 

"Embrace life."

Interpretation:
Life is precious so cherish it.

"The blind woman is deaf, but her voice is still heard."

Interpretation:
No matter your situation, never be afraid to speak out.

"Know who you are. Love who you are. Accept who you are."

Interpretation:
Love yourself unconditionally.

"Hold your dream hostage in your heart until it blossoms into life."

Interpretation:
Believe and have faith in whatever it is you want to pursue in life until it becomes your reality.

"If you're going to look over the edge, you might as well jump."

Interpretation:
Life is about taking risk. Don't hesitate.

"It's okay to be the only fish in the ocean.
More room for you to swim."

Interpretation:
When alone, you can accomplish more.

"Quality time is more valuable than expenses."

Interpretation:
It's not about how much you spend, but how much time you spend. That is what matters most.

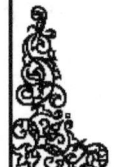

"Capture the moment, even if you have to capture it yourself."

Interpretation:
Live in the moment. Enjoy the moment even if it's by yourself.

"Cry happily."

Interpretation:
Tears don't always mean you're sad.

"Love starts with yourself."

Interpretation:
You have to love yourself first before you can love others.

"Less expectations, less disappointments."

Interpretation:
The less you expect from people, the less disappointed you will be.

"Sometimes you have to create your own melody and sing your own song."

Interpretation:
When you want things done you have to do it yourself.

"A brave man climbs the ladder expecting to fall, but a wise man climbs the ladder expecting something to be at the top."

Interpretation:
There are those who go through life with no hope or faith and then there are others who go through life despite the obstacles knowing there's something in store for them if they keep striving.

"You can't find your way through a tunnel of darkness without a flashlight."

Interpretation:
In order to get through obstacles and tough times, you have to be able to (despite the situation) smile, be joyful, be happy and think positive.

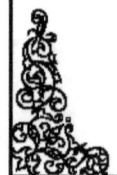

"Someone else's belief in you is ten times stronger than the belief in yourself."

Interpretation:
We all have the ability to see the part of a person that they cannot see, to see the greatness in them that they are unaware of. So when a person sees that part of you that you cannot see and believes in it, it means a lot. It makes you believe in yourself even more.

"Listen to the inner you."

Interpretation:
Always listen to your intuition, your gut, your first mind. It'll never steer you wrong.

"Let your heart lead the way."

Interpretation:
Follow your heart.

"It's only called crazy when
it isn't understood."

Interpretation:
When you're used to ordinary, out of the
ordinary will always be questionable.

"Imagination is nothing but a thought that hasn't been brought to life yet."

Interpretation:
Be in tune with your creative thoughts.

"Free your spirit."

Interpretation:
Live happily.

"Your first mind is the best mind."

Interpretation:
Go with your gut. Don't ignore it.

"Be the author of your own story."

Interpretation:
Don't let others dictate your future.

"With a smile, nobody ever sees the pain."

Interpretation:
When you stay in a good spirit despite your issues, it's hard to tell you have any.

"Motivation and progression
is the key to greatness."

Interpretation:
Success takes a lot of hard work and
determination. You have to want it.

"When life throws you curveballs, take the hits and stand tall."

Interpretation:
No matter what hardships life brings, don't let it knock you down.

"Sometimes no response is
the best response."

Interpretation:
Don't let a person bring you out of your character, walk away. Silence hurts more than words.

"Live your life like you're the only one in the world."

Interpretation:
Live the way you desire.
Live happily and free.

"Treat others like you
know them already."

Interpretation:
Treat people the way you would
treat your family.

"True friends are like blue jays
and red robins; it's very rare you come
across them."

Interpretation:
Real friends are hard to find.

"Have a heart like a lion, mind of an owl, and a voice of an angel."

Interpretation:
Be brave, wise, and kind.

"Run the race as many times as you need until you master first place."

Interpretation:
Try as many times as you need to.
Don't give up!

"Life is like a system set up to test your strengths and weaknesses."

Interpretation:
Life throws things at us to see how we will react. Hard times happen to see how much you are going to fight back without giving in. Life happens for us to build ourselves up, not knock ourselves down.

"If they can't contribute to your life today, don't try to be in their life tomorrow."

Interpretation:
Let go of those who don't benefit your life.

"It's the ones that know you the least, that help you the most."

Interpretation:
You never know who you will need in the future, and you'll be surprised with who's willing to go out of their way for you. Be kind to strangers.

"Don't second guess your best."

Interpretation:
Always have faith in yourself.

"Give yourself what you deserve."

Interpretation:
Don't settle for less.

"Life is what you make it."

Interpretation:
The choices you make create your reality.

"Be your own advisor."

Interpretation:
Listen to yourself more often, it's always easier to give advice to others, not realizing if we follow our own advice, we'll end up in a much better place in life.

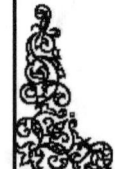

"Wake up every day like it's payday."

Interpretation:
Wake up happy, it's worth it.

"Finding yourself is like taking a road trip to a place you've never been."

Interpretation:
Once you start exploring yourself and digging deep within to find out who you truly are, you start to notice things about yourself you didn't even know existed.

"Don't create a lion you can't tame."

Interpretation:
Don't create a person or situations you can't control.

"Defeat the difficult."

Interpretation:
Overcome the hardest situations first.

"If a person cannot accept you for who you are, it's their loss, not yours."

Interpretation:
You are great the way you are. Never change your personality for someone else.

"The validation you need looks at you in the mirror every day."

Interpretation:
When it comes to yourself, your opinion is the only one that matters.

"You are your biggest fan."

Interpretation:
No one is going to support
you the way you will.

"Don't just do it for fun,
do it because you love it."

Interpretation:
Do things with a purpose.

"Somebody in this world needs you, keep striving."

Interpretation:
Don't give up.

"Can't doesn't exist."
(Inspired by my Mom)

Interpretation:
You can do anything you put your mind to.

"Go three extra miles if you have to."

Interpretation:
Do whatever it takes.

"A child is your creation
and God's blessing."

Interpretation:
Children come from us, but they're also a
gift from God.

"Success is the best way to repay your guardians."

Interpretation:
There's no way you can ever give back all that your parents, grandparents, etc. have done for you. Your success is enough for them.

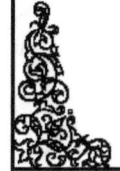

"Skate in the snow."

Interpretation:
Get through terrible times with a smile.

"Self-love matters."

Interpretation:
You must love yourself first before you can love others.

"Become the change, then
create the change."

Interpretation:
You can't change anything unless you
change yourself.

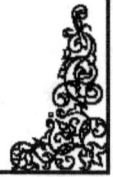

"A master doesn't reveal his plans."

Interpretation:
Keep your greatest plans to yourself.
No one has to know. The results will speak
for themselves.

"Fill yourself with gratitude."

Interpretation:
Be grateful every day of your life.

"Sometimes things aren't lost, they just haven't been found yet."

Interpretation:
Things aren't always what they seem.

"Don't become a part of someone else's world to the point you start to unrecognize yourself."

Interpretation:
Don't lose yourself trying to fit in someone else's life.

"Only expect the promises you make to yourself."

Interpretation:
Count on yourself because you won't let yourself down.

"Your mindset exposes your true self."

Interpretation:
You are what you think.

"Express yourself without hesitations or regrets."

Interpretation:
Be YOU!

"Don't cry over spilled milk, clean up the mess with laughter instead."

Interpretation:
Find humor even in the bad moments.

"Don't let situations take over you, you overtake the situations."

Interpretation:
Be strong!

"You're not always going to find people with the same heart as you, but when you do come across some, hold on to them."

Interpretation:
There are still a lot of good people in this world.

"Grandparents are special people."

Interpretation:
Grandparents carry a different type of LOVE.

"Trends of fashion eventually go out of style. Knowledge and wisdom will NEVER go out of style."

Interpretation:
Material things don't last.
Knowledge stays.

"A crippled woman is no less than a blind woman who can walk, and a blind woman is no less than a crippled woman who can see."

Interpretation:
What you have or what you don't have doesn't make you any more or any less than anyone.

"Prayer doesn't only change things, it changes people."

Interpretation:
Prayer changes situations, but it also changes people for the better.

ABOUT THE AUTHOR:

New York-bred. Loves to read and write. Also writes poems and spoken word pieces.

Shatora Gaskin, Born in East Meadow, N.Y. Raised in Hempstead, N.Y. Graduated from Hempstead High School (Top ten in my class). Oldest out of three siblings. I have a younger brother and sister. I've always loved reading and writing. I'm a huge fan of poetry. Started writing poetry when I was in 4th grade and been writing ever since. Currently employed at Adelphi University. Besides writing, I enjoy being a single mother of two beautiful girls.

www.ingramcontent.com/pod-product-compliance
Lightning Source LLC
Chambersburg PA
CBHW052159110526
44591CB00012B/2013